Setting the Tone – Decreasing Discrimination in the Workplace

Setting the Tone – Decreasing Discrimination in the Workplace

Copyright @ Creative Performance Solutions, LLC

2023

All rights reserved. No part of this workbook may be reproduced or transmitted in any form or by any means without written permission from the author.

Published and distributed by PCT Publishing

PO Box 383

Goshen, NY 10924

845-294-7089

ISBN 9798866041244

@Creative Performance Solutions, LLC

Setting the Tone – Decreasing Discrimination in the Workplace

Introduction

Today's global workforce is diverse and complex. There is no room for discrimination, yet it exists, consciously and unconsciously.

This workbook is a resource for participants who attend a professional development training program focused on reducing discrimination in the workplace, behaving in a consistent appropriate manner, and being a role model for others. After all, leaders need to lead and influence others.

Learning Objectives

We are all lifelong learners and there is always an opportunity to improve. Choosing to make improvements is your choice, you can select a growth mindset and be open to new ideas or you can move forward with a fixed mindset and pretend that you know enough. Adults learn when they want to, not when their boss sends them to mandatory training.

One of the objectives of this training program is to have fun, the other is to increase awareness about diversity, inclusion, discrimination, bias, and your behavior.

During this interactive training program, participants will:

- Define and explain various forms of discrimination, including racial, gender, religious, ethnic, disability, LGBTQ+, and age.

@Creative Performance Solutions, LLC

Setting the Tone – Decreasing Discrimination in the Workplace

- Increase their effectiveness as positive role models for others.
- Model appropriate, professional communication.
- Be exposed to microaggressions and increase awareness of inappropriate language.
- Implement strategies for increasing cultural awareness in education.
- Provide information about available support and resources that can assist with discrimination-related issues.
- Mentor others and hold employees accountable for identifying and removing discrimination.
- Recognize stereotypes and different types of personal biases and regulate behavior.

What are the challenges of eliminating discrimination in NY?

Setting the Tone – Decreasing Discrimination in the Workplace

Today's Workplace

There are five generations in the workplace.

What are the biggest changes that you have seen in NYS education since you began your career?

Good   Not so good

@Creative Performance Solutions, LLC

Setting the Tone – Decreasing Discrimination in the Workplace

The Law

Federal Law

- EEOC Title VII of the Civil Rights Act of 1964,
- Age Discrimination in Employment Act (ADEA)
- Americans with Disabilities Act (ADA)

These federal laws apply to employers with 15 or more employees.

NY State Law

New York Human Rights Law (NYHRL) prohibits discrimination based on age, race, color, national origin, sex, gender identity or expression, sexual orientation, marital status, military status, disability, and other protected categories. The NYHRL applies to employers with four or more employees.

Sexual Harassment Prevention In 2018, New York State implemented new requirements for preventing sexual harassment in the workplace. Employers are required to adopt anti-harassment policies, provide training, and take steps to prevent and address harassment.

Equal Pay Laws: New York has implemented laws to address pay equity and prohibit wage discrimination based on gender.

NYC Law

New York City Human Rights Law (NYCHRL): If you work in New York City, you are also protected by the NYCHRL, which provides even more expansive protections against discrimination. It covers additional categories, such as creed, citizenship status, and pregnancy, and applies to employers with at least four employees.

It is illegal for employers to retaliate against employees who file complaints about discrimination or harassment.

Bias

Bias is natural. Everyone has bias.

Think of the people you like to work with. What is the reason for your comfort?

Think of the people you would rather not work with or are uncomfortable with. How could you increase your comfort level?

Setting the Tone – Decreasing Discrimination in the Workplace

Types of Bias

Match the bias with the definition.

Unconscious	We like people who have a name like ours.
Affinity	We believe over achievers will always come out on top.
Halo effect	We believe people with a lot of letters after their name are smarter than others.
Confirmation	We tend to judge something or someone by making comparisons.
Contrast	We tend to prefer attractive people.
Ability	We look for data to confirm what we believe.
Appearance	We like people who are like us in some way.
Name	We are not even aware of our learned attitude and belief about something.
Religious	We prefer people who were born in the same country, village, town as we were.
Cultural	We tend to prefer people who practice the same religion as we do.
Education	We believe disabled people are not able to do certain things.

@Creative Performance Solutions, LLC

Emotional Intelligence

In 1995, Daniel Goleman wrote a book titled Emotional Intelligence. The book suggests that having a high IQ is not the only trait that leads to success as a leader. After all, there are plenty of people with modest IQs and no college degrees that have acquired extraordinary success. In his book, Goleman describes Emotional Intelligence (EI) as having five parts:

- ✓ Self-awareness – the ability to recognize and understand your moods, emotions, biases, and drives as well as their effect on others.

- ✓ Self-regulation – the ability to control or redirect your impulses especially when they are negative or disruptive. The ability to think before you act, to maintain professionalism, and at times to keep your mouth shut.

- ✓ Motivation – a passion to work for reasons that go beyond money or status.

- ✓ Empathy – the ability to understand others.

- ✓ Social Skill – the proficiency to build relationships and influence others.

The first three parts of Emotional Intelligence have to do with you. How you perceive yourself, how you decide to regulate your behavior, and whether you are self-motivated. Most leaders have a healthy degree of self-motivation or grit, the ability to move through the obstacles and focus on the goal at hand.

Setting the Tone – Decreasing Discrimination in the Workplace

Stereotypes and Prejudice

A stereotype is a widely held but oversimplified and generalized belief or idea about a particular group of people or things. Stereotypes are often based on assumptions, prejudices, or limited information, and they can be either positive or negative. These preconceived notions are typically not based on individual characteristics, behavior, or qualities but are instead applied to an entire group.

Stereotypes have been around forever. Those of you that grew up watching Archie Bunker and The Jeffersons heard stereotypes every day on prime-time television.

How many stereotypes can you think of?

1

2

3

4

5

6

7

8

9

10

Are the stereotypes positive or negative?

Often, discrimination is based on a stereotype or ignorance. We don't even know what we don't know!

Microaggression

Microaggression is a subtle and often unintentional form of discrimination. Microaggressions can vary in their form and intensity, but they all share the common feature of marginalizing or demeaning individuals based on their identity, often in subtle and unintentional ways. Recognizing and addressing these microaggressions is essential for fostering inclusive and respectful environments in schools and other settings.

Racial Microaggressions:

- Assuming a student of color must be on a scholarship or affirmative action program.
- Commenting that a student "speaks so well" for their racial or ethnic background, implying surprise at their articulateness.
- Asking a Black student where they are "really" from, suggesting that they are not truly American.

Gender Microaggressions:

- Interrupting female students more frequently than male students during class discussions.

Setting the Tone – Decreasing Discrimination in the Workplace

- Telling a male student to "man up" when they express vulnerability or emotion.
- Making comments that suggest that certain roles or activities are only suitable for one gender, like saying "girls can't do math."

Sexual Orientation Microaggressions:

- Asking a gay or lesbian student if they've "tried dating someone of the opposite sex."
- Making jokes or derogatory comments about same-sex relationships.
- Assuming that all students are heterosexual and discussing relationships or attractions accordingly.

Religious Microaggressions:

- Telling a student from a minority religion that their holidays or traditions are strange or made up.
- Assuming that a student with a particular religious background is more conservative or traditional than they might be.
- Singling out a student because they don't participate in a religious event or prayer.

Disability-Related Microaggressions:

- Offering unsolicited assistance to a student with a disability without asking if they need help.
- Assuming that a student with a disability cannot participate in certain activities or courses without trying to accommodate them.

- Making comments that suggest a person's disability defines their identity, like saying "the blind guy" instead of using their name.

Socioeconomic Status Microaggressions:

- Making assumptions about an employee's potential or work ethic based on their family's income.

- Teasing a student about receiving free or reduced-price lunch.

- Assigning group projects that require students to spend money on materials, which can be difficult for those with limited financial resources.

Language Microaggressions:

- Speaking loudly and slowly to a student whose first language isn't English, assuming they can't understand complex concepts.

- Telling a bilingual student that they "sound so American" when speaking English, implying that their other language is less valued.

Intent vs. Impact

Did you ever say something which led to insulting another person, but you didn't intend that to happen?

Intent refers to what a person meant or intended to convey when they said or did something.

It is the internal motivation or purpose behind an action or statement, and it may be well-intentioned or benign.

Setting the Tone – Decreasing Discrimination in the Workplace

People often believe that their intent is good or harmless, and they may not realize the potential harm or offense their words or actions can cause.

Impact refers to the actual, real-world effects and consequences of a person's words or actions on others.

It focuses on how the recipient perceives and experiences those words or actions, regardless of the intent behind them.

The impact can be positive, neutral, or negative, and it is often what determines whether something is hurtful or offensive.

The key point of understanding "intent vs. impact" is that even when someone's intent is not to harm or offend, their words or actions can still have a negative impact on others. In situations where intent and impact do not align, it's essential to acknowledge the impact, listen to the perspectives of those affected, and take responsibility for addressing any harm caused. This concept is crucial for fostering better communication, empathy, and inclusivity in various social and professional settings.

Understanding terminology

- Ordinary Privilege

- White Privilege

Setting the Tone – Decreasing Discrimination in the Workplace

- Tailwinds

- Headwinds

How much do you really know?

Religion	Holiday/Holy Day	Custom/Tradition	Country practiced
Christianity			
Islam			
Muslim			
Buddhism			
Hinduism			
Judaism			

Setting the Tone – Decreasing Discrimination in the Workplace

Cultural Competence

Illegal immigrants are coming to the United States by land and by sea, escaping violence, political unrest, poverty, and humanitarian turmoil. Many will end up in New York and the children will be enrolled in the NYC and NYS school systems.

	Political leader	Unrest
Mexico *		
Haiti		
Cuba		
Venezuela		
Africa		
Guatemala*		
Honduras		
El Salvador		
Nicaragua		

@Creative Performance Solutions, LLC

Setting the Tone – Decreasing Discrimination in the Workplace

- [ ] Argentina
- [ ] Bolivia
- [ ] Brazil
- [ ] Chile
- [ ] Colombia
- [ ] Ecuador
- [ ] Falkland Islands
- [ ] French Guiana
- [ ] Guyana
- [ ] Paraguay
- [ ] Peru
- [ ] Suriname
- [ ] Uruguay
- [ ] Venezuela

Setting the Tone – Decreasing Discrimination in the Workplace

Showing Respect - Everyday Manners

Many people grew up with parents and caregivers who were positive role models and taught their children manners. The importance of saying please and thank you. Greeting people with a hello or a good morning and saying goodbye when leaving.

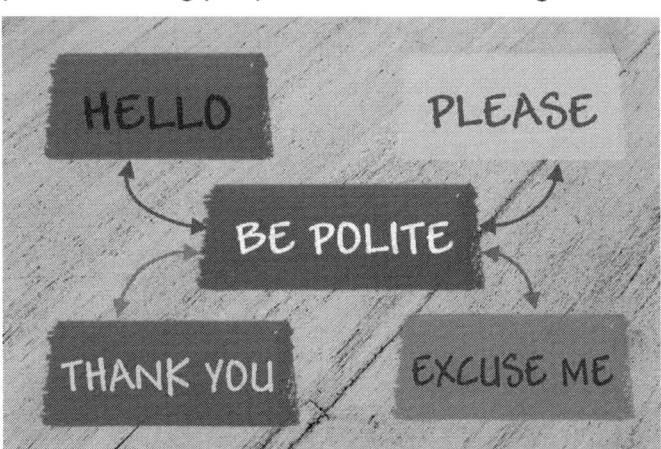

Having and using good manners is appreciated by others and shows respect. When someone holds the door open for another person or gives up their seat on the bus, it shows respect. It's a small gesture that means a lot. When a man, pulls out a chair for a woman at a restaurant, it shows respect. Quietly standing at attention when the National Anthem is being played is a sign of respect. Addressing a person with a salutation (Mr. Smith, Dr. Perez) is a sign of respect. Behaving with good manners and showing respect towards others will never go out of style.

Using appropriate visual and verbal language is also tied to being mindful of manners. When people curse, yell at others, or show vulgar hand gestures they are not behaving in a way that shows manners. Spitting, slamming doors, flipping the bird, throwing items at another person are examples of disrespectful behavior.

It seems as if every day we hear about a tragic situation where a person has crossed the line from being disrespectful to being dangerous. I have heard about fist fights between employees and other totally inappropriate behavior in the

@Creative Performance Solutions, LLC

workplace. There is disrespectful behavior all around us and leaders need to hold employees accountable and let them know that bad behavior will not be tolerated. If you ever encounter dangerous behavior in your workplace or feel threatened, call security.

What are the steps to follow when safety is a concern?

Consistently using good manners at work is the foundation to developing solid workplace relationships. No one wants to work with a rude, crude, unethical, discriminatory co-worker. Here are a few examples of appropriate workplace behavior.

- Being punctual at work is a sign of respect. Showing up on time for meetings and not wasting your co-workers' time with idle chit chat is appreciated. Pay attention to and be respectful of each other's priorities.

- When invited to a virtual meeting, sign on a few minutes early to make sure the audio and video connections work. Speaking of virtual meetings, having your video camera on during the meeting shows the person speaking that you are engaged and listening.

- Workplace etiquette should be followed while you are working remotely. No one wants to see you in your pajamas sitting on your unmade bed during a meeting. If possible, find a quiet location with good lighting to

Setting the Tone – Decreasing Discrimination in the Workplace

work remotely. If possible, keep your pets and children away from the screen. As cute as they are, they are distracting others and take time away from the meeting agenda.

- Limit your personal fundraising in the office. Just because your daughter is selling Girl Scout cookies doesn't mean everyone wants to buy some. Some employees will feel obligated to buy even when they don't really want to.

- Do not bring office supplies home for your personal use, it is stealing.

- When you meet a new person, it is polite to make eye contact, say hello, and introduce yourself. Before COVID, a handshake was a customary greeting. Today, a nod or fist bump works. When you shake hands, connect palms and shake. Don't overdo the shaking and don't squeeze your hand. A firm grip is appreciated, avoiding the limp fish handshake. That sends a terrible message.

- If you are with another person, introduce that person also and include them in the conversation.

@Creative Performance Solutions, LLC

Setting the Tone – Decreasing Discrimination in the Workplace

- A trick for remembering names is to repeat the name after the introduction. It sounds like this.

Me: *Good morning, it's nice to meet you. I'm Regina Clark.*

Other person: *Good morning, Regina. I'm Pat Rodriquez. It's a pleasure to meet you also. I don't know many people named Regina.*

- Do not take care of personal business during work time. That is why your employer gives you breaks and lunch hours. If you have a crisis at home, take the day off and focus on your personal business. Years ago, one of my co-workers had a sick child in the hospital. She came to work and spent hours sharing her personal information and distress with her co-workers. Her co-workers were empathetic, listened to her, and supported her. After a few hours of disruption, a Human Resource professional asked the employee to go home.

Setting the Tone – Decreasing Discrimination in the Workplace

Being a Role Model

What is the first thing you notice about someone when you meet for the first time?

Your visual language speaks volumes before you even open your mouth. We communicate messages with our facial expression, clothing, posture, hand gestures, and cleanliness every day. Others make judgements about us within a few seconds based on our visual language. It may not be fair or an accurate assessment, but it is what happens.

A smile speaks volumes. It communicates to others that you like what you are doing and appreciate where you are. We link smiling to happiness; a smile is welcoming. Having to wear a mask during COVID is so frustrating because it hides a person's smile! Crying also communicates a message but can be misinterpreted. When we notice that someone is crying, that person might be sad or distressed or they might have tears of joy! I have been known to cry at weddings and in church when God Bless America is being played.

What is appropriate, professional appearance for your work environment?

Is there a dress code? Has the dress code changed during the past few years? Some organizations have outdated dress code requirements that are detailed in an employee handbook, but the dress code is not enforced. A healthcare organization in New Jersey has a rule against visible tattoos, yet during my training programs with the provider I met many healthcare employees with tattoos. When I asked the employees about the dress code, they told me that no one enforced the dress code. When I asked the Human Resource professionals about the dress code. They told me that they needed to update the handbook.

Some organizations have a dress code to communicate professionalism to their customers. Police Officers, Crossing Guards, Chefs, Medical Professionals, and Mechanics wear clothing that represents their profession.

Can you think of others who wear uniforms or specific items of clothing?

Some customers make a judgement based on how the employee looks. If a person looks unprofessional and inappropriate for the job, the customer might go elsewhere.

You are the brand, and your appearance should complement what the brand stands for. You wouldn't expect a High School Principal to wear 10-inch spiked heels, and a low-cut blouse exposing cleavage with a tight leather skirt. It's not the image we have of a professional educator. In addition to clothing, a professional appearance includes good grooming. We don't want to interact with a person who has a body odor, too much perfume, or too much cologne.

Setting the Tone – Decreasing Discrimination in the Workplace

A good rule of thumb for deciding what to wear to work is – when in doubt, don't. Save the razzle dazzle outfit for one of your outings with your friends.

Are there any items on this list that are not appropriate at your workplace?

- [ ] Tattoos
- [ ] Green, Pink, Purple Hair
- [ ] Beard
- [ ] Moustache
- [ ] Turban
- [ ] Saree
- [ ] Hijab
- [ ] Nose ring
- [ ] Gold cross
- [ ] Bangle bracelets
- [ ] Open toe shoes
- [ ] Short shorts
- [ ] See through blouses.
- [ ] Strapless blouse or strapless shirt
- [ ] Hats
- [ ] Flip flops
- [ ] Sneakers
- [ ] Jeans
- [ ] Hoodies
- [ ] Athletic wear (tights pants, tank tops, sports bra)
- [ ] Colored nail polish
- [ ] Shirts with logos or statements
- [ ] Crop tops (shirts with belly button showing)
- [ ] Clothing with rips, tears, and holes

@Creative Performance Solutions, LLC

Setting the Tone – Decreasing Discrimination in the Workplace

Would you have an unconscious bias towards any of the above clothing?

There are five generations in the workplace today. Standards have changed during the past ten years as Traditionalists (dob 1925-1945) and Baby Boomers (dob 1946-1964) retire. When Baby Boomers started their career, there was no such thing as business casual or remote work. Work attire was formal back in the day and men dominated leadership positions in most organizations. My grandfather owned a grocery store in NYC in the 1920's, he wore a white, starched collared shirt to the grocery store every day. Men in that generation wore suits and ties if they went to Yankee Stadium or were lucky enough to board an airplane.

Today, the largest generation in the workplace is the Millennial generation (dob 1977-1997). Today's workforce is globally diverse, standards have relaxed a bit, and what is considered acceptable today might not have been acceptable 20 years ago. Some employers are struggling with acceptable dress code standards as the workforce changes.

In most instances, employers are required by federal law to make exceptions (reasonable accommodation) to their usual dress code rules or preferences to permit applicants and employees to observe religious dress and grooming practices. For more information, go to https://www.eeoc.gov/laws/guidance/religious-garb-and-grooming-workplace-rights-and-responsibilities.

One thing will never change and that is the expectation of being well groomed, positively representing the brand, and having good manners.

Professional Communication

Communication has two parts, sending a message and receiving a message. Often, we think we are communicating but we are just sending a message without knowing for sure if a person is receiving or getting the message. Did you ever leave a message for someone on their voicemail or email because you wanted to avoid having dialog? Did you ever have a misunderstanding because you assumed that someone received and understood your voicemail or email?

What gets in the way of effective communication at work?

Effective leaders have fabulous communication skills and usually serve as role models for the rest of the organization. There are two parts to becoming an effective communicator.

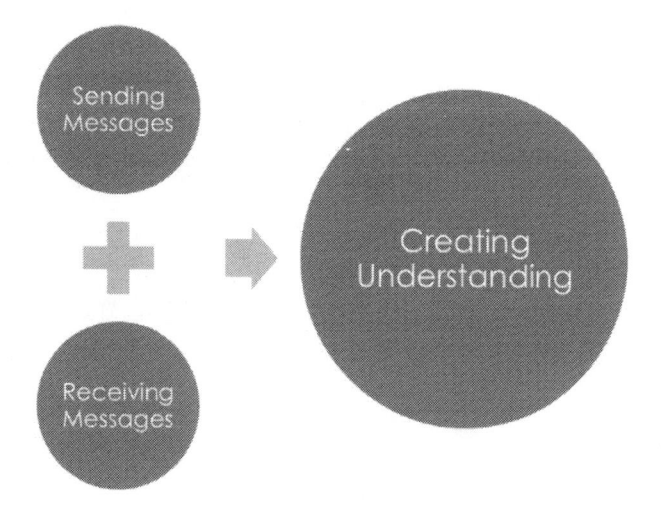

Sending Messages + Receiving Messages → Creating Understanding

@Creative Performance Solutions, LLC

Setting the Tone – Decreasing Discrimination in the Workplace

Effective communication is creating understanding between two or more parties. Communication becomes challenging when people speak English as a second language and when people are distracted by other issues and are not ready to receive the message. Just because we send a message, doesn't mean the message was received and understood.

Sending the message can be accomplished in a variety of ways:

- Speaking – formal or informal, large group or small group, in person, on the telephone, videoconferencing, webinars, via social media

- Writing – memo, email, report, book, texting, etc.

- Visual messages – body language, sign language

How do you send most of your messages?

Albert Mehrabian PhD.[i] conducted a famous communication study years ago. Mehrabian established a classic statistic for the effectiveness of spoken communication:

- 7% of meaning is found in content - the words that are spoken, or what you say

- 38% of meaning is paralinguistic – how you sound. Your rate of speech, inflection, articulation, vocal variety, and resonance impact how you sound.

- 55% of meaning is visual language – what you look like. Your facial expression, hand gestures, posture, clothing, and grooming impact your visual language.

Statistics don't make sense in all types of communication, but they are certainly something to think about. Content is critical – but so is the way you sound. If a leader has brilliant content and a monotone voice, no one will pay attention. If a leader has good content, a pleasant voice, and looks like a kook, the listener might not take him or her seriously. Effective professionals have good content, pleasant sounds, and tones, and look appropriate for their position.

Use Appropriate Language

Every profession has its own jargon, acronyms, and slang. Educators talk about magnet schools and inclusion. Lawyers talk about quid pro quo and depositions. Doctors talk about scripts and consults.

Americans use phrases that don't translate well or don't mean anything in other languages. For example, a Catch-22 situation, getting to first base, it's between a rock and a hard place, or what's up?

What jargon and acronyms are used at your job?

When you use language that the listener doesn't understand, there is a possibility that you might confuse the listener. People usually don't like to admit ignorance. They won't ask what something means. Instead, they will miss the point or interpret the message in the wrong way. Effective communicators adjust their language for the audience, they do their homework and prepare their remarks before getting in front of a podium or in front of a person.

@Creative Performance Solutions, LLC

Setting the Tone – Decreasing Discrimination in the Workplace

Use Positive, Powerful Language

Replace negative words with hopeful, positive words. There are so many negative messages in today's world. The media and newspaper sensationalize negative news. So many people complain and use consistently negative words (no, never, unfortunately, don't, can't, won't).

Tell the reader what you can do, not what you can't do.

Tell the listener what will work, not what won't work.

Tell your co-workers how to fix the problem instead of complaining about the problem.

Becoming a polished, positive, professional communicator takes practice.

In this exercise, replace the negative words with positive, hopeful words. Do not change the meaning of the sentence.

John is not here today.	
That's not my job.	
We can't meet that deadline.	
My co-workers will never agree to that deadline.	

Setting the Tone – Decreasing Discrimination in the Workplace

I have no idea how to help you.	
This place is a disaster.	
The school is closed on that date.	
We don't have any funds to invest in that project.	

Receiving the message also happens in a variety of ways:

- Active listening or listening for understanding. People tend to listen to who they want to when they want to. Adults can pretend they are listening when they are not really paying attention to the speaker.

- Reading a book, text, email, or post.

- Watching a video, social media post, or television.

Setting the Tone – Decreasing Discrimination in the Workplace

Levels of Listening

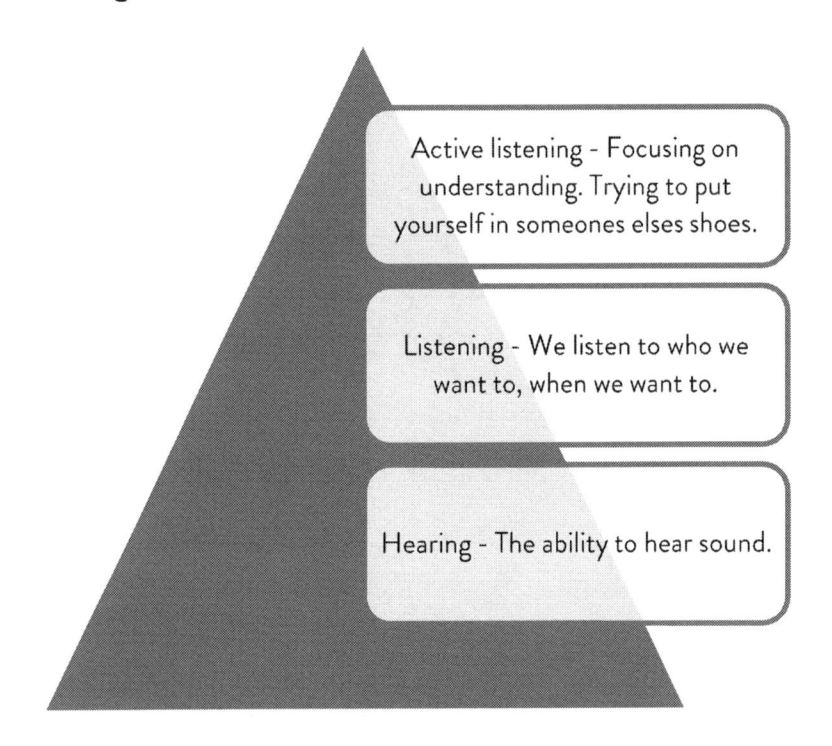

- Active listening - Focusing on understanding. Trying to put yourself in someones elses shoes.
- Listening - We listen to who we want to, when we want to.
- Hearing - The ability to hear sound.

Do you have co-workers who you would rather not listen to?

Do you tune out when someone speaks with an accent?

Do you have family members who you would rather not listen to?

What is the best way to get you to listen?

@Creative Performance Solutions, LLC

Case studies

Case # 1

A parent visits the school building and is admitted into the office. When he gets into the main office, he starts yelling about a Physical Education teacher who made inappropriate comments on his daughter's Instagram account. The PE teacher is also the coach of the girls' varsity cross country team. The parent is livid and want the PE teacher fired.

What is your next step?

Case # 2

You work in the main office. You have been at the school for 15 years. There is one co-worker who is always gossiping about the teachers. Yesterday, she shared confidential information about a teacher's health issue. You think she crossed the line.

What is your next step?

Case # 3

One of your co-workers is always eating at her desk and making a mess. She leaves wrappers and paper cups all over the place. She is getting on your nerves. She arrives at the last minute during the workday and is always the first to leave. She is constantly talking about how many months are left until her retirement. You have heard some of your co-workers make fun of her behind her back.

What is your next step?

Setting the Tone – Decreasing Discrimination in the Workplace

Case # 4

One of the staff members wears a hijab. She is a competent, lovely co-worker. A parent calls the office and tells you that he doesn't want his child in any class where anyone is wearing a hijab or turban on their head. Then he starts to yell about the Twin Towers being hit on 9/11 and doesn't anyone have any respect for America anymore.

What is your next step?

Case # 5

There is a new family in the neighborhood and English is the second language. The parents walk into the school building to get information about registering their children for school. They do not understand English. What do you do?

Case # 6

Create your own difficult situation.

Setting the Tone – Decreasing Discrimination in the Workplace

Moving Forward

1. Be aware of your own biases and behavior.
2. Regulate your behavior to avoid discrimination. (IQ vs. EQ)
3. Improve your cultural competence and support refugees and immigrants.
4. Be a role model for others.
5. Use gender neutral language.
6. Educate others.

What else?

Setting the Tone – Decreasing Discrimination in the Workplace

Resources

Do's and Taboos of Using English Around the World Roger E. Axtell

Do's and Taboos of Body Language Around the World Roger E. Axtell

https://www.learningforjustice.org/moment/supporting-students-immigrant-families

https://www.hudsonvalleyrbern.org/

Setting the Tone – Decreasing Discrimination in the Workplace

Things You Should Never Do at Work!

1. Take credit for someone else's work.
2. Behave rudely.
3. Cut your toenails.
4. Floss your teeth at your desk.
5. Yell at your co-workers, customers and/or boss.
6. Bully, harass, or intimidate others.
7. Watch YouTube videos.
8. Curse.
9. Pout when you don't get your way.
10. Tell offensive jokes.
11. Invade a co-worker's personal space.
12. Kiss, hug, and touch co-workers who don't want to be touched!
13. Make private, personal calls during working hours.
14. Look for another job while you are working.
15. Use drugs and/or alcohol.
16. Eat a co-worker's food.
17. Look through a co-worker's desk.
18. Fist fight.
19. Gossip.
20. Take a nap at your desk.
21. Complain, no one is interested.
22. Lock doors to prevent others from leaving.
23. Urinate where you are not supposed to.
24. Sneak a cigarette in the bathroom. This is not high school, grow up!
25. Make a mess.
26. Insult others.
27. Damage company property.
28. Take home office supplies that do not belong to you.
29. Plan a personal function on company time.
30. Use a company vehicle for personal errands.
31. Waste time viewing and posting to social media.

@Creative Performance Solutions, LLC

Setting the Tone – Decreasing Discrimination in the Workplace

32. Hide your pet in your office.
33. Undress.
34. Have sex.
35. Be unproductive. You are getting paid to work!
36. Sabotage others.
37. Share confidential information with the wrong people.
38. Discriminate.
39. Retaliate.
40. Throw things.
41. Roll your eyes at your boss.
42. Get drunk and/or wear provocative clothing at the holiday party.
43. Order the most expensive item on the menu at a company function.
44. Eat all you can eat if you go to an all you can eat buffet with co-workers.
45. Slam doors.
46. Sell company furniture on Marketplace.
47. Post pictures of your co-workers online.
48. Post negative comments about your employer online.
49. Handle a family crisis at work. Take a personal day to deal with family issues. That's what they are for.
50. Use your workplace to store personal belongings.
51. Keep moldy, smelly items in your locker.
52. Be consistently late.
53. Nurse your baby when you are conducting a performance discussion with one of your employees.
54. Share your political and religious beliefs and opinions. You are paid to perform a job function, not to preach to others.
55. Display inappropriate signs, banners, or flags in the workplace.

Setting the Tone – Decreasing Discrimination in the Workplace

Notes:

Setting the Tone – Decreasing Discrimination in the Workplace

Additional Training Programs

Communication
- ☐ Assertive Communication for Women
- ☐ Interpersonal Effectiveness
- ☐ Spice Up Your Speaking
- ☐ Secrets of Superb Facilitation – not on site
- ☐ Dos and Don'ts of PowerPoint
- ☐ Storytelling to Increase Engagement – new description, not on site
- ☐ Engaged Listening
- ☐ Email Etiquette
- ☐ Creating Your Professional Brand
- ☐ Business Etiquette

Management Development
- ☐ Management Made Easy
- ☐ Time Management for New Managers
- ☐ Coaching and Counseling
- ☐ Behavioral Interviewing
- ☐ Conducting Performance Discussions
- ☐ Dealing with Difficult Employees
- ☐ Managing Conflict
- ☐ Secrets to Managing Meetings
- ☐ Introduction to Process Improvement
- ☐ Tips for Restaurant Managers
- ☐ Sexual Harassment Awareness for Managers

Leadership Development
- ☐ Effective Leadership
- ☐ Using Assessments to Increase Leadership Effectiveness
- ☐ Leading Multigenerational, Diverse Teams
- ☐ PIVOT – Conquering Change
- ☐ Employee Engagement and Your Bottom Line

@Creative Performance Solutions, LLC

Setting the Tone – Decreasing Discrimination in the Workplace

- ☐ Developing Your Replacement

Customer Experience
- ☐ Creating WOW Customer Experiences – not on website but have description
- ☐ Dealing with Difficult Customers and Challenging Situations
- ☐ Improving the Customer Journey
- ☐ Customer Service on the Telephone

Healthcare Customer Service
- ☐ Improving the Patient Experience
- ☐ Leading the Patient Experience
- ☐ The Physician Leader
- ☐ Dealing with Difficult Patients and Challenging Situation
- ☐ Communication Skills for Healthcare Professionals

Workplace Productivity
- ☐ Managing Your Time
- ☐ Maximize Your Productivity
- ☐ Balancing Deadlines and Diapers

Other
- ☐ Train the Trainer
- ☐ Train the Six Sigma Trainer
- ☐ Team Building
- ☐ Is Your Net Working?
- ☐ Sexual Harassment Awareness
- ☐ Workplace Safety & Violence Prevention
- ☐ Creative Problem Solving

@Creative Performance Solutions, LLC

Setting the Tone – Decreasing Discrimination in the Workplace

About Regina M. Clark

Regina M. Clark, CSP is a sought-after international speaker, author and founder of Creative Performance Solutions, LLC, a leadership development consulting firm which she started in 1994 after leaving the corporate training world. For most of her career, Regina has been helping leaders and teams improve their performance. Regina is a professional member of the National Speakers Association who received her Certified Speaking Professional designation in 2005, a designation held by less than 10 women in New York State. She is also a SHRM approved speaker, a DDI certified trainer, a certified virtual trainer, a distributor for Wiley and a NYS certified MWBE. Regina has spoken to audiences in 40 states and five countries about process improvement, improving the customer experience, being a better manager, delivering effective training programs and a variety of other topics. To learn more about additional training programs, visit www.reginaclark.net or call 845-294-7089.

End notes

---

[i] Professor Albert Mehrabian has pioneered the understanding of communications since the 1960's. He received his Ph.D. from Clark University and in 1964 commenced an extended career of teaching and research at the University of California, Los Angeles. He currently devotes his time to research, writing, and consulting as Professor Emeritus of Psychology, UCLA.

@Creative Performance Solutions, LLC

Made in the USA
Middletown, DE
18 August 2024